Graceful Wings

by

Janet O. Maddix

Compiled

by

Mark A. Maddix

ISBN-13: 978-1533466556
ISBN-10: 1533466556

DEDICATION

In memory of my mother,

Grace

For my children and grandchildren

INTRODUCTION

Poems bring meaning to our lives because they evoke deep emotions. These carefully crafted stories speak to our hearts.

Poetry is a rich form of literature that uses rhythmic qualities of language to express meaning. They are designed with specific forms and structures that include verse and syllable patterns. This book is organized around more traditional poetic categories such as limericks, sonnets, free verse, and prose.

This book includes a collection of poems written over many years by a gifted poet—my mom. Throughout my life I have watched her creative gift and imagination to pen poems that are reflective of her experiences. Her poems are woven from the scenes of nature, times with family, and her faith in God.

As you read these poems you will gain a greater glimpse into my mom's life as a child growing up in a large family in rural Kentucky. She speaks of her father and nature, her mother; trees and daffodils, the kitchen chair, and Olive Hill High School.

She also writes about life events such as the Fourth of July, Presidents, the magic of Christmas, traveling to New York City, and enjoying the Nevada landscape. All of these experiences are representative of her ability to see meaning in the rhythmic patterns of life.

She has titled this book "Graceful Wings" building on her previous two books "Spirit Wings" and "Wordwings." "Graceful Wings" has special meaning to mom because it is dedicated to her mother, Grace.

Graceful Wings reflects the attitude and characteristics of my grandmother, Grace. They also are embodied by my mom who continues to live a life of grace with a deep faith and compassionate love for people.

In this book mom has given us an opportunity to experience graceful wings! Enjoy!

Mark A. Maddix, June 15, 2016
Nampa, Idaho

CONTENTS

Sporadic Memories

On a cold and snowy day
I find nothing better to do
Than gather old pictures and poems
    From hiding places,
    Rescue them,
Remember when they were new.
It is like finding buried treasures,
Photos that missed an album,
Memories from moments well-spent.
    Living and loving,
    Believing, trusting,
Greeting each day with surprise.
Our children's children
    As years disappear,
Grow up before our eyes.
Pictures from billfolds or off the frig,
    No chronology here,
    Just sporadic pages
To satisfy my appetite for hobby-lobby rages.

Freedom

Freedom is a poem
released on graceful-wings
from my soul to yours.

Lyrics

"Evoke a musical quality in sound and rhythm,
describing the poet's innermost feeling."

I Picked a Poem from a Tree

I picked a poem from a tree
an Irish ode enchanting me.
I saw the strength within this verse
to build a heritage of worth,
a family tree of lyric lines
to scan the years and so define
the generations that would grow
from seeds of thought fallen below.

I picked a poem from a tree
and found some words reflecting me,
ancestral songs and lullabies
from ages past to future ties.
The patterns followed through the years
are truly procreated here.
With amazement and delight
I clutch my poem and hold it tight.

Snowflakes

As shimmering ice crystals
fall to the earth
we watch
we wonder
we reflect
we are filled with mirth.

Snowflakes
each so unique
yet clinging together
they form a peak
or mound
or slanted roadway
where children play
and scream with laughter
on their sleigh.

Snowflakes
nature's winter gift
arrive in splendor
to awe us
to enthrall us
to give us a lift.

Growing up in the Country

I remember while growing up
drinking water from an old tin cup,
water drawn from the well outside
carried to the kitchen with pride.

There was a rocker by the old fireplace;
a dinner table was spread with lace.
We milked the cow each morning and night,
a kerosene lantern gave us light.

We strained the milk in country crocks,
carried wood for the old wood box,
molded butter in a wooden mold,
a flower on top, big and bold.

We slept upstairs in a feather bed,
sister at the foot, me at the head;
said our prayers at the end of day
thankful for another day of play.

For my Grandsons

My grandsons and I stood beneath my tree
now aged and gnarled like arthritic me.
Beyond the field, we played in the creek,
skated rocks on the water, gave the landscape a peek.
From the bridge, what a view!
My childhood home under skies of blue.

Sixty years ago Dad planted a tree
in our family yard, a tree just for me.
I watched it grow year after year,
sat beneath it in summer eating roasting ear,
feeling proud that Dad thought enough of me
to take the time to plant that tree.

Now sixty years later I have a family tree;
as I watch it grow it amazes me.
The fruits of the branches, some girls, mostly boys
are a heritage to me, bringing much love and joys.

Blossoms of Sunshine

When springtime beings to blossom
and Resurrection Sunday is near
I think of the beautiful flowers
that grow in our gardens each year.

The tulips are colorful welcomes
to this season of hope and new life;
lilacs and violets in purple
are groomed and ready to thrive.

The jonquils are anxious to greet us
as they toss golden heads in the air;
the crocus comes whispering promise
that winter is gone, spring is here.

Of all the buds that blossom to bloom
and brighten the winter-worn earth
one is outstanding and lovely;
He gives to this world a rebirth.

On the mountain He is Rose of Sharon;
in the valley, a Lily so fair;
in my heart, blossoms of sunshine
to bloom with each answer to prayer.

Summertime Pleasures

Before the summer days are fully gone
I want to make a few more jars of jam
and eat fresh melon from the wilting vine.
I want to picnic by a shallow pond
and watch the fish swim in and out the rocks
as quiet hush invades the cool evening.
I want to hang the wash outside to dry
in summer's wind and past the red roses
giving aroma to the drying sheets.
Before the summer days are fully gone
I want some memories for a winter day.

A Kentucky Housewife

My mother was a Kentucky housewife
who had great talent for design.
She often sewed on her treadle machine
making garments that would be mine.

When I was in need of new clothes
for school or a country show
she would send me to the general store,
and I was always anxious to go.

I could choose a colorful pattern
from the supply of chicken feed sacks
for the ensemble I would be wearing
when the chickens had finished their snacks.

My Grandmother's Feet

I remember my Grandmother's feet;
they were short with stubby little toes,
and when she relaxed in her rocker
they were covered by long heavy clothes.

She would often have me wash her feet
at the end of the hard-working day;
with a granite washpan and towel
I would kneel down as if to pray.

When I stroked her hard callosed ankles
she gently patted me on the head.
"What would I ever do without you?"
I remember the words that she said.

Not long ago at the end of the day
my granddaughter bounded in the door.
I quickly asked her to wash my feet
since my ankles were hurting and sore.

She gave me a look of absurdity;
my request came as a surprise.
Afterall, with modern facilities
why ask for a pan and supplies.

When my feet were relaxed and soaking
I placed my hands on her head.
"What would I ever do without you?"
I repeated what my Grandmother said.

11

Memories of Fourth of July

We were walking down the street on the Fourth of July
when my mother asked me what I want to buy;
"Nothing, really," was my reply.

The street sales were fun just looking around
and talking with folks who had come into town,
not to mention the parade and humorous clown.

My mother and I had a hotdog to eat,
then a brownie for something sweet
when I spied a Rattan vase up the street.

Mom sensed my interest in the tannish brown vase
and asked the price as she fingered some lace.
"Five dollars, not a bad price, huh, Grace?"

"I'll take it!" Mom said as she gave it to me,
"You keep it or pass it down the family tree."
Did she know this would be our last shopping spree?

I've treasured my vase for many years
and now when I dust it, my eyes fill with tears;
that gift from my mother will forever be dear.
On the Fourth of July when parades come to town
I go and I laugh at the funny clown
and always the presence of mother is found.

A Place in Time

A PLACE IN TIME reads the sign next door;
unique, the shop is an antique store.
People flock there from far and near
to search for treasures of yesteryear.
An old cream can sits near the door
reminiscent of the days of yore
when cows were milked each morning and night;
the home had a cream can somewhere in sight.
Old wooden ironing boards standing tall,
hand irons and wire trivets near the wall,
blue mason jars for canning of food
and wash boards like my mother once used.
A primitive froe and a turning plow
take me back to the hillsides and how
my father cultivated the rocky land
and patiently split the fence rails by hand.
All these are reminders of another time,
pieces of the past put together in rhyme.

Personification

"Verse in which inanimate or non-human

objects are given human attributes."

Quixotic March

Third sibling in a diverse family,

unpredictable and moody,

quixotic March makes her entry

with storms and blustery winds

like a lion.

Born with a split personality,

this frustrated child

defies the ides of her birth month;

she thrives

on promise of pussywillows

and wild flowers in the woodland,

the first robin of spring,

and the awakening

of bears and chipmunks.

She supervises northward flights

of wild geese and ducks,

chides prophetic April ills,

then leaves with a smile,

sunny and mild

like a lamb.

Morning Glory

They say I am a temptress
        who lures with subtle charm
invading the forsythia
        although I mean no harm.
When the sun comes up each morning
        my colored blossoms roam
in and out the planted shrubbery
        by the structure I call home.
I have a sensual nature
        liberated, roving free,
yet I bloom a very short time;
        this is fair, you must agree.
There are times I am not welcome;
        I admit this is a fact,
and I will avoid clematis;
        she and I have formed a pact.

Thoughts of a Kitchen Chair

My ladderback is humped and heaved
    from years of strain and use.
My seat of rush is dropping out;
    it has suffered much abuse.
They use me for a stepping stool
    when things are out of reach,
and every week I hold the kids
    while sister tries to teach
the spelling words and capitals;
    I know them all by heart.
And every morning I hear prayers
    that give the day a start.
When the family comes to breakfast
    I smell the fresh-made bread.
The father grabs me for a seat
    and places me at the head.
Sometimes I am forced backwards
    by a prankster for a joke;
I feel badly when someone falls
    and I cringe at what is broke.
My place beside the radio
    keeps me current with the news;
Grand Ole Opry on Saturday nights
    helps with the week-end blues.
When my usefulness has ended
    and nostalgia ups my worth
I will move to antique heaven
    for renewal and rebirth.

Old Sewing Basket

Where have I been these many years?
Stashed away....forgotten....useless?
When I was new, a secret gift to you,
my cushioned backing had purpose.
You stored every loose button you found,
safety pins, and all colors of thread,
needles, stick pins, rick-rack and tape
and trimmings for your bed.
Oh, the times I saw you thread a needle
to sew on buttons or mend a tear.
With my lid wide open, you'd pause
to remember a friend or say a prayer.
I hope my service to you will last
as I hold stitched memories of the past.

Corn Husker

In my young days I was rather handsome
when my leather straps were new;
the hardware stores had me on display
advertising what I could do.
A farmer who was raising a corn crop
came to town for some staples one day,
said his corn was about ready to husk;
he bought me and took me away.
For years I worked for the dear farmer
faithful upon his strong hand,
but as he and I began aging
we just couldn't harvest the land.
My owner went into retirement;
I was sold to a quaint antique store.
My straps were aged and corroded;
not fit to be used any more.
A family came by on a journey,
stopped by the old store just to look;
the children were curious about me,
what use are these straps and sharp hook?
The father decided to buy me;
now I live in a nice modern home;
the children have learned of my usefulness
on the farm where their ancestors owned.

Blank Verse

"Unrhymed iambic pentameter-
Poems can have as many lines as you want."

Under the Quilting Frame

I used to play under the quilting frame
and listen to my mother as she talked
with neighbor women who came by to help.
The conversation that I heard became
the morning news and neighborhood concerns.
My view was quite distorted when I saw
some legs that dangled on cane-bottomed chairs
and thimble fingers reaching from each form
to needles moving in and out the cloth.
My small domain grew smaller day by day;
then like a migrant soul, I moved my things:
a cigar box of hopes and dreams of life.

Florence Nightingale

Her life began in elegance and wealth
entertaining royalty, kings and queens.
She could not shut her eyes from all the pain
within the London slums; it proved too much
to tame her zealous soul filled with distress
each time she saw the poverty and woe.

She believed her life was a splendid gift
with faith in God and service to humanity,
that character is built from works of love:
Don't think Ideals but do the Father's will.

Until she was allowed to be set free,
she was a captured eagle behind bars,
her wings beating on the family cage.
No holiday or game could satisfy
the quest to heal, which was her love of life.

A good Samaritan to wounded men
her nursing skills achieved reform and fame.
Longfellow penned: "The lady with the lamp
brought light and hope of healing to the world."

Villanelle

"six stanzas with five triplets and a quatrain."

Come and See the Picture I Took

Come and see the picture I took;
Four children were having such fun.
Their faces should be in a book!

The picture captures a happy look,
Smiling faces bright as the sun.
Come and see the picture I took!

It is hanging in the breakfast nook
And quite impossible to shun.
Their faces should be in a book!

I look at it each time I cook,
A photograph second to none.
Come and see the picture I took!

I laughed at this scene until I shook
And labeled it "Grandmother's Pun."
Their faces should be in a book!

All pride and manners they forsook
As they ate boiled eggs and a bun.
Come and see the picture I took!
Their faces should be in a book!

A Winter Storm is on its Way

A Winter storm is on its way
expect to have high winds and sleet
the weatherman forecast today.

It was a shock to hear him say
we should get snow, two or three feet;
a winter storm is on its way.

An excellent time to read and play
or clean the house to make it neat
the weatherman forecast today.

It could be fun if power will stay
to snuggle by the fire and eat;
a winter storm is on its way.

Bring in some wood without delay;
you need a fire to give some heat
the weatherman forecast today.

Be sure to pack your cares away;
just pop some corn, prop up your feet;
a winter storm is on its way
the weatherman forecast today.

Limericks

*"A humorous, frequently bawdy, verse of three long
and two short lines rhyming aabba"*

Limerick

A woodpecker pecking on a tree
Stopped his pecking and looked at me
When he stopped his drumming
I stopped my humming
I think we were in the wrong key.

Limerick

There was a fellow named Darryl
Who went over the falls in a barrel;
Lost his balance in the fall
And that is not all;
He also lost all his apparel.

Limerick

In the Garden of Eden was man
With a monkey, a bear and a lamb.
There was no woman's lib
When man gave up a rib.
If so there would have been bedlam.

Sonnets

"A poem, properly expressive of a single, complete thought, idea, or sentiment--three quatrains & couplet. Each quatrain has abab rhyming. The couplet lines rhyme. The lines are in Iambic pentameter."

In Memory of Our Mothers
(Heritage of Love)

The heritage my mother left for me
transcends the early treasures she could give
but rather she bequeathed the dignity
to trust and love and honest ways to live.
The fibers of my soul are so entwined
with all the lessons taught me through the years
that now her very presence seems defined
in daily tasks and when I'm facing fears.
I know my mother prayed for me each day
to be successful and find happiness
and on this Mother's Day I too will pray
for strength to be a mother who will bless.
I want the love my mother had for me
to be passed on to all my family.

Nature and My Dad

I watched a famer plowing in his field
and instantly a picture came to mind;
I saw a hillside farm intent to yield
the corn and beans to feed our family nine.
My Dad with his old horse and shovel plow
would stagger through uneven rows of corn
just pausing long enough to wipe his brow
and gaze around the farm where he was born.
I think my father had a fellowship
with earth and sky, a oneness giving peace,
a needed faith to sow and then to reap;
our livelihood depended on increase.
Reflecting on this scene from ages past
Provides me with an image that will last.

The Magic of Christmas
(A grandmother's observation)

On Christmas Eve when all the world was still
they sprinkled magic oats upon the lawn
in faith as legends say that reindeer will
arrive with Santa at the crack of dawn.
My heart is stirred to see this youthful play,
the innocence and fun of fantasy;
I only wish the older folk today
could view the world and see as children see.
For if we looked at life the way they do
each day would bring a new surprise;
our child-like faith would stand to see us through,
no matter what we face, what may arise.
The Christmas story comes alive each year
as children with the magic help us hear.

The Bible

The traveler will lose this way without it;

The pilgrim needs this staff to walk upright.

It is a compass for the soaring pilot,

A sword for soldier's fighting in the night.

It is a lamp with paths to direct us,

Tasty food supporting hungry souls.

Its comfort cheers the person who will trust

And believe the precepts it unfolds.

We read the inspired words for consolation,

A history book containing only truth,

The state of humans, the way of our salvation,

A charter for the old as well as youth.

This book of books gives life to all who read

And hope to all believers who will heed.

A Lone Tree

A lonely tree stands in an open field,
the only landmark left on this farm site.
I think of secrets that could be revealed
from this old tree. The countless tales of night
as weary farmers rest beneath the stars.
Perhaps by day the tree gave needed shade
to caravans traveling from afar;
they find repose, a sanctuary made.
A boundary marker, the lonely tree
may be exposed to lightning in a storm
and take the strike. The heroism shown
by stately trees bare scars upon their form.
If you travel across the country side
you can expect a lone tree still alive.

My Music Mentor

(For my Sister, Lois)

I know someone who loves to play guitar;
she strums and chords with passion from her soul
and celebrates with children near and far
the music she has breathed for years untold.
She loves the blend of voices with the strings
and teaches every child who wants to learn
creating joyous harmony that brings
euphoric blessing to her in return.
There is no doubt her talent is innate,
as well, the spirit of all her caring;
she truly wants through love to demonstrate
the extreme joy our lives can have in sharing.
I am the protégé of her good living
inspiring me to practice much more giving.

Humorous

"Light Verse-Poems that attempt to be humorous,

brief, on a frivolous subject."

The Love Bug

I'm in love with a yellow bug

one I can hug

when my heart cries

or trouble lies.

This love bug will let me hear

what I hold dear

comforting songs

to right my wrongs.

My romance with the Volkswagen

leaves me draggin'

the body's too small

and I'm too tall.

Thirty-third President

Why do I feel akin to Truman?
What can we possibly have in common?
Let's see!
He was friendly and full of charm.
Can I claim these virtues?
What about this?
We both grew up on a farm.

Um! Kentucky and Missouri:
Not too far apart.
He loved the piano, Chopin and Mozart
In the National Guard,
he rose in the ranks, like my husband
For nine years driving the tanks.
When he ran for President in '48
As a child, I thought it great
To witness his whistle-stop campaign.
HE CAME THROUGH OLIVE HILL!!
At the town depot, I saw him
His daughter Margaret as well.

Our political parties clashed.
Only partly?
He did have a Kentucky Vice, Alben Barkley.

Outdone by Technology

Technology has outdone me this time;

to get some gas I got in the line.

With credit card in hand I reached for the hose;

a signal warned me NO SALE, out of gas I suppose.

But no, I must insert my card

to activate the pump;

lift the nozzle, insert the hose,

no response, another hump.

The gas attendant came running to see

what was wrong.

It seems my card was wearing a scratch;

she said I had used it too long.

Now we are back to number one;

just pump the gas and pay when you are done.

Mouse

We've been outsmarted by a mouse.
It is true! We have evidence!
There has been a mouse in the house;
He nibbles on the bread, and hence,
Leaves droppings all around.

This culprit robs me of my space,
Where to house my crackers and bread;
We set a trap, and yet there's no trace
Of where the intruder tread
Except for droppings all around.

After weeks of pursuing that "you know who"
We are getting desperate, furious.
We must resort to those traps of glue,
Place them where he will be curious,
See if the droppings are found.

Now we have to be patient and wait
Just hope we find him trapped or dead;
Will the little fellow meet his fate,
While consuming his last taste of bread?
Clue: no droppings were found.

Old Man Fishing

I'm an old man now
　and can't do much
Cept tend my garden
　and gin and such.
Just wonder where
　the years have gone;
They swept away
　my strength and song.
Guess I'll wake tomorrow,
　take a walk in the sun,
Gather my fishing gear
　before the day is done.
Head for the waterhole
　down by the barn;
Spend some time with the fishes,
　spin them some yarn.
What a tale I'll have
　to share with them,
If I can get to sleep
　and dream a good dream.

Self-Image

I made my world;

I knew the risk

of kindness shown

and love imposed.

I chose to give,

to live for others,

sacrifice my wants and needs.

You see me well

although

the image I see

is left to quell.

Haiku

"A Japanese form-three lines poem with seventeen
Syllables, written in a 5/7/5 syllable count."

Haiku

Red and brown splashes
coloring Kentucky hillsides
Paint an autumn scene.

Snowflakes fall to earth
as shimmering ice crystals;
Natures' winter gift.

Springtime's refreshing rain
Quenches the earth's winter-worn thirst
To waken new life.

Clear blue summer skies
infuse my soul with reflection
A spirit of hope

Haiku

Autumn leaves falling
flutter like gold butterflies
lighting on the ground

Haiku

Crystal white snowflakes
Land gently on the windowpane
Painting a winter scene

Haiku

Beret-capped acorns
falling from tall stately oaks;
offspring of autumn.

Haiku

Lanterns in the night
lighting the path of darkness
flickering fireflies.

Prose

"Written in paragraphs rather than verse, but contains the characteristics of poetry with meters, with a focus on images,"

OHHS

I walked into the renovated gymnasium of my
Alma Mater. There it was, the same stage
where I stood 60 years ago getting ready to
graduate. I walked across to get my diploma
in the presence of my teachers and family.
This same spot where "The Darling Brats" was
performed. I was one of those brats that senior year.
The maroon and white curtains sparked a song....
'On You Comets' as memories bombarded my senses.
I could hear the clapping at pep rallies, the
singing of choral clubs, the sound of band instruments
tuning, making mixed harmonies. I could see the
classes filing in from the side doors, taking seats
in the bleachers waiting for the principal's instructions.
The history of OHHS is part of my history, I walked
proudly inside to celebrate the restoration of
Olive Hill High School.

Childhood Days

The large painting has been in my dining room for
decades. The local frameshop owner chose a picture
just right for us, he said. Childhood Days by Sottung.
I've dusted the antique frame many times, served
dinner in this room not thinking much about the scene.
Recently I was drawn to it as if my spirit willed me
there. The Victorian house in the distance is hedged
with prairie grass and imprisoned by weather-worn trees.
One tree with its gnarling limbs and darkened trunk
is encircled by children, three girls and one boy. I missed
the story jumping out at me!   My children!
A little boy with brown hair, two girls with red hair, and
another girl, the daughter we didn't get to keep, who now
dances in the painting with her siblings.
The innocent, simple joy of Childhood Days
blesses me and reminds me of the privilege of being a
Mother, to know a lonely house welcomes the dancing
feet of children.

Epitaph: A Beautiful Life

(In memory of my nephew,

Jeffrey Layne Smith)

What can I say about someone whose memory

    is etched in my soul?

It began in London, Kentucky; we traveled there

    with Grandma Grace one day,

    December cold.

In the hospital we waited, anticipated

    this miracle of life,

    excited to be told,

"It's a boy!" Another son to join the four,

    a precious life added to the fold.

How can I, with pen and ink, express how

    through the years this gentle giant,

    meek yet bold,

lived life to the fullest, companion to his

    brothers, devoted to his parents and his Lord,

In high school and college, in duty to his

    country, in marriage and fatherhood.

"A man is measured by his friends,"

    a famous quote once heard

    was exemplified when Jeff died.

Friends came from far and near to remember,

    to honor, to revere

A beautiful life.

Triolet

"A French poem form composed of eight lines. Its rhyme scheme is ABaAabAB and often all lines are in iambic tetrameter: the first, fourth and seventh lines are identical, as are the second and final lines, thereby making the initial and final couplets identical as well."

The Groundhog

Surveying from his winter home
    with squinted sleepy eyes
he peers for shadows on the loam
    surveying from his winter home.

A wise and curious little gnome
    weather prophet in disguise
surveying from his winter home
    with squinted sleepy eyes.

Spiritual or Inspirational

"The root of "spirit" means to breathe. Spirituality brings forth breath--opening our hearts to ponder about God and God's activity in our lives and the world."

Wait Upon God

I take a lesson from the eagle
When he is ready to fly;
He patiently waits for an updraft
To help him soar in the sky.

When I am spurred into action
to achieve my goals day by day,
I wait upon God for direction;
He always shows me the way.

The House of God

There is a haven for the heart to dwell
within the House of God each time we pray.
The roof is rainproof and the walls are strong;
the Father never turns us away.
We step through the door, walk boldly inside,
then ascend by our thoughts up the stairs.
Worshipping here we can touch the king's throne
leave with Him all our worries and cares.
Our prayers are honored as precious perfume,
a fragrance moving upward to Heaven.
God listens intently, our spirit can rest;
we are welcomed, our sins are forgiven.

A Kentucky Redbird

A cardinal flew across my path today.
He perched beside the road as if to say,
"Your day is blessed, be happy on your way."

When day was done, I bowed my head to pray
In thankfulness for such a lovely day.
A Kentucky redbird colored my skies of gray.

Forgiveness

In quietude

my soul breathes peace,

accepts what is,

prepares for what can be,

and lets go of the past.

Warm satisfaction

anoints my life,

and I sigh relief.

A Mountain Woman

She grew up in the mountains of Kentucky
Scratched out a living off the land
Walked barefoot, survived hard times
Suffered stings on her callused hands.

Pine Tree Resin and mutton tallow
Served as her balm of healing salve
Herbs and roots were made into tonics
Homemade remedies was all she had.

The land provided food for her family
A gristmill ground corn into meal
Potatoes were holed up in the winter
Hogs in cold weather would be killed.

A mountain woman used her mind
To create fun and games for play
Grapevines to swing on, stick ponies to ride
Lightning bugs at the end of the day.

In spite of all her hardships
She found comfort in her faith
Trusted God for His provision
And for her household to be safe.

Cinquain

"A five-line poem known for simplicity, vivid in imagery and conveys a mood or emotion. The syllable count is 2/4/6/8/2."

Winged Flower

Golden
day-time creature
propels its thin body
in and out the butterfly bush:
winged flower.

Oil Wells

Oil wells
on Kansas Plains
bowing, rising, lifting
harnessing underground power
fuel.

Dark Clouds

Dark Clouds
casting shadows
on vast desert landscapes
will entice the parched sagebrush plants
below.

Summer

Summer
slips away through
the door of September
ushering in the cool days of
autumn.

Rondeau

"A short poem of 15 lines with two rhymes throughout; the first four words are repeated twice as a refrain."

The Ides of March

The month of March is like a game
that never leaves just as it came;
the strategies from day to day
affects the rules by which you play
and often render you as lame.

It may arrive with voices tame
to give us days that are the same,
or with her violent winds portray
the month of March.

I frankly think it is a shame
to taunt her style or mar her name;
despite her ides she makes the way
for spring to come with its display
and this alone brings her to fame:
the month of March.

The Daffodils

My daffodils in morning frost
succumb to cold, bright color lost.
Their April life was short indeed,
yet in the ground the sleeping seed
gives promise for new life embossed.

Each morning I became engrossed
with nature's beauty without cost,
priceless pleasures fill every need:
my daffodils.

In autumn when the ground was mossed,
the flowers fading, brown leaves tossed,
my thoughts of spring gave way to greed,
embellished passion to succeed
with planted bulbs, this first accost:
my daffodils.

The Day I Shopped

The day I shopped, some things I bought
were not on the list I brought.
So much on sale how could I relent
to stock up on condiment
just think of the savings wrought.

The store receipts, transaction caught
reveal my purchase without thought
and shows me where my money went
the day I shopped.

I try not to be distraught;
this happens rarely, I was taught
when shopping, to have intent
and follow the list lest money spent
will stretch the budget for naught
the day I shopped.

The Mardi Gras

The Mardi Gras is held each year
in prominent cities far and near.
I'd like to be a traveler there
and celebrate the carnival fair
with common customs we hold dear.

The flocking crowds will shout and cheer
as floats and marching bands appear
in fancy dress and masks, they will share
the Mardi Gras.

At this festivity you will hear
the jazz of the south, and you'll be sure
to feast on great food served with a flair
in fancy restaurants, nothing to spare
an American tradition will long endure;
the Mardi Gras.

The Redwood Trees

The redwood trees grow very tall
with systems that are rather small;
to bear their great weight, I am told
the roots are interlocked and fold
in such a way they cannot fall.

Together they grow to form a wall,
the oldest and largest trees of all,
a fortress strong enough to hold
the redwood trees.

Once on vacation I do recall
how we linked hands and began to crawl
around the foot of a tree so bold;
it may have been two hundred years old,
these towering giants that we call
the redwood trees.

Free Verse

"Poem length is free without any stanzas,
and most often without rhyme."

The Spell of Daisies

Near my childhood home
I walk down the country road
on a cool mountain afternoon.
The old maple tree
still stands
where once I carved
myself into history.
In a field near the creek
tall slim poplars
witness my nostalgia
as I fall under
the spell of daisies:
"He loves me!"
For a moment,
I am the child who grasped
this rainbow of hope.

The Simple Life

I am sitting at the kitchen snack bar
with a cup of coffee and newspaper.
I can hear the hum of the dishwasher
and clothes dryer.
The television is on,
news about the presidential race
and a recent plane crash.
The telephone rings,
A tele-marketing call.
In the morning paper,
a column about the Amish lifestyle,
a simple life.
No electricity, no plumbing,
a vanishing way of life.
I recall my childhood,
no electricity, no plumbing,
no television, no telephone.
A wonderful life.

Nevada Landscapes

Traveling across Nevada,

my passenger-view is like a panoramic movie

canvassing the vast sandy desert lands,

with a backdrop of snow-capped mountains

framed against the sky.

Sporadic patches of white alkali flats

blend with sagebrush plants and cacti

to create blurred splashes

of stripes, streaks and spotted patterns

speeding parallel with me.

Bighorn sheep graze on jagged plateaus that

glow red in the sunshine

as I feed on nature's glowing handiwork.

Reading the Refrigerator

Early in the morning while making coffee

I am distracted by the wealth of faces

on my refrigerator. I stop

and spend a few moments remembering and reading

stories of every shape and size.

A nephew's new baby, birthdays, weddings,

a travel card from my son,

photos from children and grandchildren,

nieces and their families,

sport events, prayer chains.

Subtle literature, oceans of prose,

Beckoning readers, young and old.

The refrigerator…

a fireplace of the 21st century,

warms hearts,

draws visitors to its welcoming chapel.

I hear the hum of the frig….

I smell the fresh-made coffee….

I move away from morning solace.

Remembering New York City

On a ferry,

Returning from the Statue of Liberty,

a New Yorker recommends an eating place

Carnegie Restaurant,

Sounds impressive!

We took a subway,

arrived, stood in line,

enjoyed the view of celebrities' pictures

along the wall.

Finally, a table for us, a shaky table.

A bowl of pickles,

the waitress, the order, the wait.

Food at last on dirty plates,

but we were famished; we ate.

Today I'm watching Regis and Kathie Lee,

in New York City,

in Carnegie Restaurant,

in the same corner where we sat,

at the same shaky table.

A bowl of pickles (hope they are fresh);

Regis is getting impatient;

I now recognize the waitress!

Food at last!

Why aren't they eating?

I Think of You, My Mother

At summer's end when days are long
and leaves wither on the vine
I think of you, my Mother.

I think of the cool evenings we spent
on the old porch swing listening to
nights sounds, the nonchalant chirping
of crickets, the low-hoarse croaking
of frogs, and Saturday night barking
of Dad's hound dogs chasing a fox
on the distant hillside.

I think of our view from the porch,
the swaying hay fields ready for
harvest, the corn fields and potato
patch that needs to be reaped.
I remember my mother's words,
"It's about time we dug them potatoes
and put them in the cellar for cold
winter days."

Memories linger….time passes….and
each autumn, the season I last saw you,
I think of you, my Mother.

ABOUT THE AUTHOR

Janet O. Maddix is a retired elementary education teacher and active member of the Carter County Poetry Society. She and her husband Amos have three children, seven grandchildren and three great grandchildren. She enjoys reading, crossword puzzles, playing the piano at church, and spending time with her grandchildren.

She is also the author of other poetry books including "Spirit Wings" and "Wordwings." She is a frequent user of Facebook and would welcome your friend request.

Made in the USA
Monee, IL
10 October 2022

15554606R00046